Teardrops and Smiles: My Journey of Healing

Ursula Lampley Jones

AuthorHouse™
1663 Liberty Drive
Bloomington, IN 47403
www.authorhouse.com
Phone: 1-800-839-8640

First published by AuthorHouse 5/22/2009

ISBN: 978-1-4389-5743-2 (sc)

Printed in the United States of America
Bloomington, Indiana

This book is printed on acid-free paper.

Dedications:

This book is dedicated to anyone who has ever believed that once you have faced your darkest hours the light will shine again, to anyone that has ever had to face their darkest fears alone to awaken and be grateful for the journey they had to endure. I commend you and wish you the best. Many prayers and much love.

I am honored that God has allowed me to continue to write my experiences in this book. This is in honor of my family and friends, which have been priceless to me. I would especially like to honor the late Martha "Nina" R. Jones and Henry Jones, Sr., Miguel Davis, a wonderful person who gave me the confidence to always believe in myself, and Jaiden Henderson, an extraordinary young man who will one day change the world.

Table of Contents

Prologue:

My life is not perfect. I am not perfect. I will never pretend that I am. There was once a time when I believed that I had to be everything that everyone else thought was best. Yet I was the person who knew what was best for me. It was up to me to make my most sacred dreams into the reality that I knew they could become if I believed.

I have had many blessings in my life as well as many hardships. I have been more fortunate than most, yet not as happy as I desire. This is my reality.

Everyday I will strive to get a little closer to the dream I see for my life. I know that I will constantly be having good days and bad days, yet I will never give up the hope that I can be happy. Being happy is a constant state of mind, which is not always possible.

Throughout the collection of poems, you will see the good, the bad, and the ugly. There were times when I did not recognize the person in the mirror in front of me. But this was necessary to get to where I am today.

Without the downfall, there would not be the success. Once I hit the lowest place in had in my life, I realized that there was nowhere to go but up. That is my hope for you as well.

Reflections:

Why when we are in a crowd do we still feel the most alone when we are sad?

If the world is to become a better place, the first change must begin from inside of you.

Why when so many people are searching for their true love is it the hardest thing in the world to find?

It amazes me that life can so quickly change from unbearable to content and on the road to happiness in a matter of time. It goes to show that God can do anything if we just believe and trust in Him.

When we try to hide the truth from ourselves, we are only denying that joy, freedom, and beauty that comes from self-acceptance.

When we stress, we think we are holding on. But when we let go of our pain, that is the moment that we become truly free.

The beauty and love that God expresses to us through nature is priceless. Stop and see His wonders.

Although life is often filled with unexpected turns, daily trials and tribulations, it is a constant reminder for me to remember that I am not of this world. God has a plan for me, something better than I could have ever designed for myself. Believe this for yourself as well, and our lives will become less stressful when we realize that we each have a special Divine purpose.

Dear God,

Please come and take the pain away. I still see many crying from the hurts of yesterday.

Why do I feel so all alone? Carry me and take me home!

Through the ups and downs of life I know the journey's just beginning... With you by my side I plan on winning!

Not giving in to fears and doubts... But discovering truthfully what it's all about...

Sometimes when it rains it pours... And I feel like I can't take it anymore!

But as long as we are here we'll be put to the test: refined, shaped, and molded until we're at our very best.

Dear God,

I woke up this morning, my heart filled with dread. Yet I remember the promises you said would guide me through life even as I cry... You'll keep me alive when inside I want to die.

I often wonder why tragedy hits so close to home...it could be worse, I tell myself, yet my broken heart feels so alone.

Sometimes I want to give up, to just throw in the towel... Stop running the race before it's begun, yet you show me how.

You've saved my life so many times and I often wonder why... When I thought I would fall somehow you made me fly...

You love me so much; I'm not special at all...just an ordinary girl who took a fall.

Yet no one in this world is quite like me... You said I'm an angel, that I'm your masterpiece...

Still I don't understand why love was given and taken away

Is he the one for me? That is what I often contemplate

Yet I know the truth will all be revealed in time... I just feel so impatient - my life's out of line

You tell me to take care of me and Lord I'm trying to

Yet my heart longs for that special love - what am I to do?

I've gone through heartache before and I'm tired of these games!

I'm ready for the sun to shine, to stop being out in the rain

The only way I can get through this pain and truly be whole again

Is to let you guide me through and help my heart to mend

I'm not yet where I want to be, yet still not where I was before

So I truly know you'll guide me through that open door

Each day walk with me and help me to grow strong

To heal the pieces of my broken heart and figure out where I belong

I know that everything happens for a reason

And someday it won't be rainy for all seasons

Please bring miracles in my life

And answer my prayers and make my dim future so bright

I know someday you'll send me The One

Yet there's much that must be done

So although I want to give up, I'll let you lead the way

To heal my heart and send me brighter days

Love's Lessons

Love has taught me many things: hurt, pain, betrayal, despair, forgiveness, but most of all, faith. Without the many painful experiences I have endured, I would not be the person that I am today. It has led me to realize just how precious I am as a person and what I have to offer someone else as an individual.

Love Divine

Two worlds apart, yet you're still in my heart

All of these emotions - just don't know where to start

You touched my heart nearly three years ago

While love has been chaotic and life just seems to flow

The characteristics I seek of my one true love

Sent from God from up above

Yet doubt lingers on like a wound that won't heal

Are we too different? I don't know how to deal

I long to find our common ground

And to hear the beat of your heart pound

Yet only God know what the future holds

I don't know what I'm doing in this life but here goes!

Here goes everything and the parting of my heart

Has been given to you so don't tear it apart!

God guide my way to my true love

Let your will be done - send him from up above

Love Defined

Who are you? Do I love you or hate you?

Long for you or despise you?

I long to feel your touch yet will you away with all my might

As my heart wishes you held me tight

The love that keeps me grounded and insane all at once

You make me feel both old and young

The weakness of my soul and the happiness in me

My other half, can't you see?

I am yin and you are yang

My heart heard the blues when it sang

The apple of my eye and the fire in my fury

Are you for me? Let's ask the jury

Back and forth I go between mind and soul

So hard to push you away and to let you go

You're everything I need and nothing I expected

I fear my heart will get rejected

You once promised me the world

Then gave your heart to another girl

Yet you are here again - we both made mistakes

Still I'm not sure how much my heart can take

I long to live a life with you

But can you make my dreams come true?

We've gone full circle against the test of time

Will you ever truly be mine?

You are the love of my life and the bearer of bad news

Now it's up to me - which path will I choose?

It's hard to say - when I try to let you go

I can't let you go away - the truth only God knows

Love and Loss

When things hit you hard like a blow to the heart

They can instantly tear your world apart

Yet as you cry your tears, know you're not alone

The love of God is always near to make you feel at home

I know because I've loved and lost so many times it seems

And I still have yet to find the man of my dreams

Although I long for true love it is my time

To grow within myself and make my future mine

I cannot deny my feelings - I know God hears my pleas

As I feel His unsurpassing love bring me to my knees

I am in love with someone not meant for me

Yet the feelings are slowly fading - I finally can see

Now I truly know that everything I desire

Will be fulfilled by God as He sends me inner hope, passion, and fire

My journey's just begun and I know it won't be easy

I'll still have hard times that turn me from warm to freezing

Still God has worked a miracle in my life

When I thought I wouldn't survive through the night

So someday I'll truly find the one God made just for me

Until then I'll still enjoy my life - to heal and be set free

Reflections in Life

One of the hardest things to do in life is to let go of someone you love

But sometimes that time comes when you realize they're not enough

They may abuse and mistreat you like dirt on the ground

Yet suddenly miss you when you aren't around

Or perhaps they will love you and then grow confused

Leaving you feeling as though you've been used

Your world may fall apart, your heart shatter to pieces

Yet there comes a time when you must believe

Know that what you're going through can truly heal in time

As I know you may wait for some kind of sign

Yet the most important thing for you to do

Is to realize that you deserve more and to always love you

I know that times are hard but you are in my prayers

I'm going through it too so know we all have many layers

Of weakness and strength, of loss and hope

Of pride and shame, yet we can cope

I've gone through so much to be so young

Yet I realize my journey's only just begun

I once thought my life was over but can finally see

That God has special plans for me

He has them for you if you open up your eyes and see

God's always in control and He'll make your life the way it's meant to be

Love's Disguise

Have you ever had a disguise?

That pulled the blanket over your eyes?

When you thought "The One" was finally here

You have to again face your biggest fear?

I've been scorched in the flames of love

For the second time - my heart's been played with so rough

Yet neither man had any remorse

For the deep heartache and life taken off its course

God says we must forgive one another and I have been loyal

To love one and all yet I only feel inner turmoil

For someone to turn his feelings on and off like a switch

To never shed tears or bleed from your heart and your special love to ditch

Pledge vows of eternal love then have a change of heart

How would you feel if this happened to you? Would it tear you apart?

This is only the beginning of my story - I know God will see me through

Every hurt and pain and make my heart like new

Selfish Love

Into the darkness you slither along

Following me and saying how you were wrong

Longing to confess your love, yet it is all lies

Even your name I despise

I've finally moved on - taken control of my life

Yet you insist that you will always be mine

How could I love a liar, a cheat?

My expectations you could never meet

I gave you my love for so long

Yet you took advantage and only went along

To get what you needed and lie your way back in

When all of this time you were a sin

Leave me alone! My life is my own

Control your faithful wretch you have - you seeds have been sown

Nothing you can say or do will ever change my mind

For I have my life back and it is truly divine

To be healed from loving someone selfish and untrue

When I all I ever tried to do was love you for you

Yet you are strange and unmatched for someone as great as me

I opened the door and can finally see

After loving too much twice in my life

It's time to give it to myself and heal my strife

So I've said my piece and I will stand tall

Above your lies and abuse - one day I'll have it all

Healing Myself

Once I made a wish to find the love of my life

Someone to heal my pain and strife

I used you as a crutch just to get through the day

The only thing I had left in life, yet I knew it would be taken away

Away we disappeared in a world of our own

Yet I had never felt so very alone

You had eyes but didn't see and failed to have a heart

Peering deep into my soul you dissected and tried to tear me apart

I thought I could rely on you forever

Yet we were never really meant to be together

An awkward little girl who grew into an unsure young woman

I always felt so all alone, but realize I had more love than I'd ever known

You wore a disguise - I don't know who you are

All those nights I thought you were the answer from my wish upon a star

Yet I'm finally strong enough to say, "No more!"

I'm better off without you - I'm tired of making my heart so sore

I have such big dreams and wish to fly

Yet you held me down and made me feel like I should die

I've always been strong, yet I never knew

I have enough love for myself to make my own dreams come true

My Life's Pitfalls and Struggles

Do you show a brave smiling face to the world and then let silent tears fall from your face each night? This is my duality: the constant struggle for balance and acceptance. Light and darkness, happiness and sadness, faith and despair...I still struggle with these barriers everyday of my life.

How do you overcome the depths of hell to reach Heaven? How do you maintain a compassionate heart when so many will you to fall? How do you forgive those who hurt you and couldn't care if you died tomorrow?

God doesn't promise us an easy life, but He does promise to lead us home. Joy and pain are part of the journey to complete appreciation and healing.

Accept the good and the bad within yourself, but strive to become Divine. Complete. Whole.

Dreams Away

What am I to do with my life?

So many dreams, so little time

The clock keeps ticking away

Every moment lost sends me astray

Errands to run, bills to pay

Jobs to get, no time to play

No time for things I love with all my heart

Leave me breathless and unable to finish what I start

The goal to get to where I need to be

Is to work but right now it's hard to see

When I'm getting older by the day

And I feel my talents wasting away

It's all for a purpose, yet my heart doesn't know

I'm reluctant to do tacks - I miss my music so

My dreams and goals seem so far and I am so afraid

Of the future I feel that I myself have made

I just want a chance to break free

To finally be happy - it means so much to me

With a heavy heart I finish my tasks

But I must remember that trouble never lasts

My soul is crying out to be saved

Yet I'm the one who must be brave

Continue on and soon dreams will come

With a future as bright as the sun

Afraid to Fly

Afraid to live, afraid to fly

Feeling inside like I'll cower and die

Longing to smile, to enjoy my life

Instead of fearing the morning sun - all the pain and strife

I know the path I must follow yet people say it's wrong

It's time for me to finally sing the tune to my own song

Where did it begin? From my birth

Chipping slowly away at my self worth

I'm ready to be me no matter what it takes

It's finally time for me to do things my way

Heart Apart

A heart apart, don't know where to start

I try to speak, but am silent - where is the spark?

I stare in the mirror at yesterday

Wishing the wind hadn't blown my house away

I finally returned home and then out of nowhere

I was forced to pack up my bags without a care

I'm trying to have a brave face, but I'm crying inside

I want to go back home where inside I'd find

The smiles, the tears, and memories of the past

My life as it was that I thought would always last

So now here I am: emptiness and all

Someone please catch me before I truly fall

Yet somehow I know God will make everything okay

This is what I truly hope and pray

So put me back together and give me back my life

Give me back my heart and soul and make everything alright

Story of Love, Redemption, and Heartbreak

I thought I was redeemed - I saw angelic faces

A fallen angel yet again has left heartbreak in her traces

I'm so ashamed to be here again - I was supposed to learn my lesson

It's hard to forgive myself and move on from dark sins I've been confessing

Demons haunt me in my dreams

Where nothing's truly as it seems

All I've ever wanted was true love

Yet somehow I feel I messed it up

I know God will give me many chances

And sees my heart through all circumstances

Still I feel unworthy - look at the pain I caused

How can I live with this guilt inside - this emptiness and loss?

The love of my life is gone and it's all because of me

All the love he had for me I wasn't able to see

Yet everyday I hope and pray that someday there will be a new beginning

That the storms of destruction will be gone and the calm of dawn will be rising

So Lord I'll pray every day and every night

For you to bring my true love to my side

Yet before you do, heal me first

And make me a better woman, for better or for worse

My prayer is noble, my prayer is pure

I'll be forever grateful if you can reassure

That my love and pain are not in vain

And the dreams I have are still the same

I don't know how long, I don't even know what day

I don't know the time or even what I'd say

But the moment he enters into my life

I'll never be the same - I'm meant to be his wife

God's Answer Key

Where is my life truly heading this time?

When will I see from God His sign?

To move ahead and make my dreams come true?

Are you for me and am I for you?

There's so much I want to achieve in this life

Yet so much pain still lingers deep inside

When I feel weak, I remember that I've survived

Through the worst of it all and I'm still alive

I'm heading back to the top but I'm longing for that man

The one that God made just for me - someone who truly understands

I'll keep praying and asking God for everything I need

And one day that locked door will have a key

Waiting for Greatness

Waiting for greatness to come to me

Searching for the locked door with my key

How do I contemplate all these feelings deep inside?

When from my true self I can never hide?

I remember the lost days of yesterday

When I felt my soul had flown away

Inside I felt rage and turmoil burn my blood

The tears trickled down like a flood

It's hard to let it go, the shadows of the past

To pick up the pieces of my life from thrown rocks that were cast

Yet I now see hope and a future for me

And the promise of true love that I could never see

So I'll move on, yet I'll never forget

I'm stronger now and able to reach all the goals in life I set

Turmoil of the Soul

This inner emptiness claims my soul

And on warm days I am often cold

The scars from childhood still linger on

As I look upon my future with uncertainty - I cry for days that have gone

I long for someone to take my hand

A kind friend who would understand

Yet my entire life I have pushed away

Those who wished to be close to me every single day

So in my depression I walked alone

And felt I had no friend to call my own

I have so many goals and dreams in this life

But I need someone to understand my pain and strife

I can't be perfect - I need to face the facts

To reveal the truth and stop hiding behind a mask

My fears have always been, "What if I'm not accepted?"

"For the person I am and get rejected?"

Yet I can't let fear hold me back forever

I only live once so I need to get it together

I trust God to lead me on my way

To stand through the test of time each and everyday

Journey of Pain and Healing

Four is where my pain began. And now it's where I start again.

I began a life filled with the promise of dreams.

Yet remember that beyond every smile that everything's not always as it seems

My doubt was instilled in me as a child

The ugly duckling trying to smile

My teenage years were awkward and crazy

Sometimes I feel a little hazy

I always dreamed that as an adult my life would magically fall into place

Yet nineteen is the age where I felt separate from the human race

The façade of happiness disappeared

And in its place showed all my fears

Of pain, doubt, worthlessness that had always been there

But I'd felt ashamed and that no one would really care

I was different, you see

Of what was truly expected of me

Four is my journey and four is my pain

Where an angel fell and was thrown out in the rain

Yet I was not alone, the devil was there

To feed me his lies and stop me from going anywhere

I felt so deserted, I felt so lost

I lost my self worth and thought my soul would be the cost

Going crazy from deep inside

Yet from night to daylight each day I cried

While others were resting I was confessing

Never expecting to receive a blessing

I thought I'd found love, yet had been sent the devil's son

Who planted seeds of destruction - my pain really had begun

Yet I felt so helpless - where was my savior?

I was told that I had lost His favor

Cursed by nightmares in my dreams

And the presence of evil that would never leave

All this time I thought it was in me

Or perhaps my broken family

So I left home to start a new life

To try and fix what was broken, to make everything alright

Yet I suffered abuse unimaginable in the mind

Feeling I had no where else to turn - so inward I cried

God sent angels along to aid me on the path

But every night I could hear the devil laugh

I didn't know how to escape my prison walls

Or how to hear the Lord's call

So for four long years I died

Yet was reborn again and finally feel alive

I let it all go and returned to my life

And to a family who had been there all of the time

They loved me for me yet I never knew

I saw the pain I had caused but God made us anew

I trained myself to listen and God said, "It is time."

So I gathered up my things and left my jagged life behind

I'm not all put back together - there are still broken pieces

But everyday I hear the Lord's promises that He will never leave me

So always enjoy the simple things in life

Before you run out of time

God gave me wings to fly on my own

Yet through my life He promises, "You'll never be alone."

I am God's true miracle, a true testimony to all

So if you ever need me I'm here to catch you when you fall

Message of Love

Do you know how hard it is to be who I really am?

In a world that's so cold, do you truly understand?

People hurt me and I begin to boil with wrath

But then I start to hear the devil laugh

It's not my way, despite my pain

I am kind and I am true - with hate there's nothing to gain

I want to believe that goodness exists in us all

There's God in me and God in you - don't let the devil make you fall

It's all so simple - why can't you see?

The love in our hearts will set us free

So despite all these scars I have I know God's way is right

And I'll say a prayer for all of us tonight

We need each other more than we know

To hold us together and help us grow

God is love, let it lead the way

Together today and always

Wait and See

I have often wondered if I look like I have my life together

Do I look stress free and light as a feather?

You don't see this deep pitted soul

That longs to find that one true love and never let go

I am a contradiction of sorts in my own right

A blending silhouette both in the day and the night

The truth I so often hide

Locking away what I truly feel inside

Where did this begin? Since I was young and pure

A place where I once felt so sure

Yet a wall crushed my soul and closed me in

Vowing that I would never open up again

After years of hiding, I'm ready to show

The world a different side of me they've never known

Do your emotions affect your body, soul, and spirit?

Do you fight between self-doubt and self-worth - do you long to hear it?

For so long the brightness of my soul was locked away

I secretly waited for my prince to come and make my pain dissipate

That was a mistake you see - you must put yourself first

For I am the soul that resides in this skin always for better or worse

Longing for other to notice my pain

To break the curse and pull me out of the rain

Yet I realize now that God can heal me

He can make me anew and give me everything I need

So when I wondered off on my own path I finally see

God would have done much better - He knows exactly what I need

Patience is a virtue and not one in which I'm strong

But I'm discovering now that I was truly wrong

Instead of instant gratification from love, money, or success

I caused myself much unneeded and unwanted stress!

I'll trust Him to walk with me down this unknown path

And not worry about anyone who may point and laugh

For God told me He has something special planned for me

The only way to be blessed is to simply wait and see

Vault of Silence

Do you know how hard it is to be?

The true person that is really me?

Do you know how cruel the world can look from my eyes?

A friend becomes a foe - the truth turns into lies

So when I turn to those I'm connected to by blood

They rise up my anger and cause hot tears to flood

Does anyone see I want the very best?

For us all but I'm being put to the test

So many demands, so little time

The only way to keep sanity is to look towards the Divine

So much I'll never say so I don't cause waves

Wish I could shout it all so my spirit would be saved

Fighting to be happy yet please others too

Did you know it's a struggle everyday to wake up and not be blue?

This is so frustrating - the silence I must keep

The vault is locked - to my inner soul I retreat

God will be my witness to the emotions of my heart

And keep me grounded when they try to tear me apart

All I can do is pray for better days

And do the best that I can do to meet the world that I must face

Faith through the Rain

How do you feel when secret darkness is exposed?

The doubts of your heart shown to strangers of hosts?

Would your inner light diminish if you sensed their satisfaction?

In knowing they played a part to your soul's subtraction?

I hear them laugh at me and I feel inner wrath

A longing deep inside to protect and attack

Yet God says, "Have peace and face your fears."

"I will guide your soul at ease and bring blessings so dear."

The truth is, it matters not what they think or know

You cannot let them take away the goodness of your soul

So keep on living life and be exactly who you are

Knowing your dreams will take you far

The gifts God has given no small fool can subtract

Accept your true self and with others interact

For the time is coming to blossom - can't you feel it?

Trust your faith and trust your heart: your faith in God will seal it

Reaching Out, Holding In

Longing to reach out

To make it count

Yet my doubts close me in

Make me feel like I can't win

Success and failure seem intertwined

Everything is connected - life sends you signs

Life always keeps you grounded

Searching for my soul, I finally found it

Wishing to connect to another breaking soul

My guard is up yet I will it to go

How can I even begin to describe

The secrets of my heart, the truth I feel inside?

Some days I am invincible - I can do anything

Other days I feel so small - blown away from the wind the breeze can bring

Feeling like an alien out of the world for many years

Silently holding in all my secret joys and fears

Gifts can be a blessing or they can be a crutch

Some days I wonder if life is really worth the fuss?

Yet today I piece together pieces of the puzzle

Sorting it out, looking for connections among sisters and brothers

Yet all I need God has given me inside

A strong soul and a courageous mind

The significance of life sometimes baffles me so

Yet life's experiences shall help me to change and grow

Gold is Best

In my life, it's always been about someone else, something else

What they need is more important

Being angry makes me appear jealous, selfish, or needy

But I want to know: Is it wrong to long for gold when all you ever get is silver or bronze?

Why must everything come before me?

When is it my time to shine, to play the leading role?

For so long I have never been first

It pains my heart to endure such daily turmoil

It not only destroys my ego but my soul, the very best inner part of me

Can't anyone see I need to be loved?

I can love equally in return

Somehow the silence remains

Nothing unchanged, I continue on another day

Truly Alive

Feeling so dead inside

So absent from my pride

Wasting away from my purpose in life

While I silently cry deep inside

This is how I feel each day

Praying for God to take the pain away

Beginning a foundation but lacking the passion

Feeling as though I won't have time for action

To fulfill the true calling God has in store for me

What truly makes me happy and sets my soul free

I hope God will put together the pieces of the puzzle in my life

So patience can heal my pain and strife

Longing to be free, longing to fly

Waiting for that day when I am truly alive

Silhouettes of Corruption

Silhouettes of darkness in the night

Surround my spirit and fill me with fright

I searched for true love yet found an empty seed

Corruption and disguise filled the air along with rage and greed

I was blind and I was weak

I fell so low - unable to speak

But now I am stronger and I say, "Enough!"

My heart is tired of being played with so rough

I thought you were an angel - it was a disguise

Corruption of the heart and a house of lies

Yet I will persevere - I'm much stronger now

Stick around and I'll show you how

With the Lord by my side, I am never alone

And with friends, new love, and family what has been reaped will be sown

Two Reflections of Me

The jagged mirror doesn't lie

I see two reflections in my eyes

One girl is strong and has it all

While the other feels like she's going to fall

Happiness, sadness

Contemplation, madness

To hate what you see yet try as you might

To find your way back towards the light

Don't have the time to fall - I must keep going

Yet all this time I'm knowing

I have to take the time to truly heal

In this life before I can deal

I keep running from her, from what I've become

I feel so ashamed - I long to flee from the sun

God gave me a chance to make my life right

Yet the shadows of my heart won't leave my sight

So many ambitions, so little time

So much pressure and yet I wonder why

What happened to that little girl who could do anything?

I need her strength to guide me through - to come and save me!

I locked it all away - the dreams of my heart

While my mistakes slowly tear me apart

I must learn to forgive the person who needs it the most

So this flower can blossom and finally grow

The only one who can create miracles is me

So that my spirit can be one and finally be set free

Life

In life you'll find that you'll always dream

And you'll realize that nothing's as it seems

You'll grow, you'll change

Your light will always lead the way for you

Be true and life will take you far

I know it's hard to follow your own way

Through thick and thin we all have our bad days

But I'll always be there for you, don't be blue

Just swallow your pride

Feel alive and remember

Your heart and your soul

Feel your might, watch it grow

Life is grand, understand

It's in God's hands

So nothing is lost from you

God will see you through

All your heartache and pain

Your tears and your rain

If you don't believe

How can you achieve

Happiness through hurt

Live for better or worse

You choose your path

Win or lose

Be happy or sad

Just know you can grow

When you live life for you

You'll be at peace

Your soul will be at ease

Your dreams will come

You'll shine just like the sun

Loving Me

This hasn't always been easy. Being different isn't easy. It still isn't something I always embrace. But it is my calling. God loves me just the way I am. He designed me this way. That makes me special; unique and one of a kind. Who said that was bad?

God's Promise

Used to be in such a rush to find that perfect man

Someone to hold me in his arms - someone who understands

Living with a hole in my heart

Slowly began to tear me apart

I feared my time had past - he would never come

Yet I failed to realize all the promises God had not yet done

He had meant for me to be strong - to grow bright as a star

Take my dreams and let them carry me far

God said He'd answer my prayers as long as I had faith

For so long I'd been striving to do things my own way!

Patience is the key to make it all fit together

The pieces of the puzzle I'm seeing - God's promises are forever

It's all in His time - that's what I realize

Everything will happen when He says it's right

So that love and those children are waiting for me

Right now it's time for me to open up my eyes and see

Stronger Me

Lord I'm getting stronger - can you tell me how?

The bridge I thought I'd never cross is behind me now

I'm saying and doing things I never could before

I sense your Divine power opening the door

It's okay to be human - I finally see

I am not perfect - I am only me

But that's exactly what you intended

Each day I sense a stitch of my broken heart mended

I'm finally healing! I'm so glad it's time

For me to say everything that's been on my mind

Guide me and lead me and I'll never go wrong

Forever wise, forever kind, happy and strong

Down and Up Again

Have you ever hit rock bottom? I've been there before

Fallen so far off the path couldn't take it anymore!

Longing and needing for anyone to see

The pain and weakness deep inside of me

Yet I fell even further - I was pushed to the ground

Taken advantage of with no one else around

Love yourself first - begin that journey

No matter how long it takes to reach your glory

I still have days both good and bad

And a love unlike any other I've ever had

Life is life for everyone, whether princess or pauper

I'll no longor limit the woman I'm becoming - no one can stop her!

You've got to face the heartache, the tears, and the pain

See yourself standing out in the rain

When you face your worst fear you'll see you're much stronger

Than you ever imagined - your soul is like thunder

Although life will be life and tears will come to you

God will guide you when you're down as long as you are true

Looking at Me

Always looking for direction

Couldn't ever seem to stop stressing

Feeling lost in the world around me

Searching for my guiding light to come and set me free

Finally a dream showed me the way

Guiding me back to earlier days

Remember the past but embrace myself

Reminiscent of the former girl that was once my self

After years of praying, the light is coming back

Spunk, spontaneity, serenity - that's a fact!

I'm not perfect and never will be

Yet I'm learning to accept the growing strength deep inside of me

It's time to shine! Let my light glow

Around my life everywhere I go

Looking Back, Moving Ahead

I let him go and I'm proud to say

I'm in charge of my life and having things my way

Despite the pain and heartache I learned a lesson

That life is too short to always be stressing

Love that's for you will not lead you astray

It will cherish you and grow each day

Although I've been hurt before I have faith

That true love will one day find a way

I'll guard my heart more closely yet always be

The true, real authentic me

All the anger and the hurt, I've let it go

Because it's time for me to grow

For now on I'll be number one in my own life

Happy and someday be a special man's wife

Obligations of the Heart

Trying hard to see the light

To have the courage within to win my fight

Pressures surround me from all around

Relentlessly knocking me to the ground

So much to do - no time for me

I keep pressing on yet I see

The underlying stress that plagues me each night

Keeping me awake no matter how I try

When it comes time to do what I love

My energy is gone - it's not enough

It seems so unfair yet I don't want to let down

Everyone who needs me around

What is the truth? Where does my joy lie?

As I search deep in my very own eyes

Although I have days both good and bad

One moment I'm happy and another I'm sad

I'm searching for the key to finding me

Yet the answer is inside - I must set it free

My Heart's New Beginning

A new life, a new start

A new beginning for my heart

Loving myself is precious beyond words

As I hope and pray for all I deserve

Following my heart - please lead the way

As I pray I will not be lead astray

No matter where I go in life I'll always have me

Never again will I settle - I'll set my soul free

Life is what I make it - that's how the story goes

As God knows my potential and beauty far beyond the rose

I count my blessings each and everyday

And to God I'll never forget to pray

A glow of radiance upon my face

Is more precious to me everyday

Much time from happiness has been lost

Yet I have so far to go - I'll be my own boss

The element of surprise I begin to surmise

As time passes right before my eyes

I have so much to say - yet there is time

God will lead me to my destiny and what is truly mine

Difference in Me

The difference between me now and then

I was once unsure but now on myself I depend

The world was once a mystery

Now experience has shown me what I once couldn't see

I was afraid of it all - to go for my dreams

Yet nothing is ever as scary as it seems

I was once my own island, never needing anyone

I've come to realize that we all need someone

I pretended hurtful feelings were not there - I didn't think anyone would care

Expression is my philosophy of life to make my burdens as light as air

I settled for it all, being half of myself

Too afraid to dream I left my feelings on a shelf

Now I'll have it all or nothing - it's what I deserve

I am now strong enough to know what I am worth

Blessings of Today

A new days is dawning, my future is so bright

Yet I can never forget those haunting endless nights

In order to be free, I must let go of the past

And focus on the present where my dreams have been cast

To appreciate blessings of today I recall countless nights of doubt and fear

And the heartless destruction of all I hold dear

Yet I've been given a second chance in life

A time to redeem myself and make things right

I never thought I'd get here, thought I'd been held down forever

Yet with the Lord of God, never say never

Divine Perfection

Perfection I am not, so I no longer try

To live my life with no mistakes or to never cry tears from these eyes

I accept what God has made in me

For it's the only way to be happy and free

It wasn't always this way - let the truth be told

I haven't always been vivacious and bold

The woman standing before you today

Was built from experience - I have much to say

This glowing pride, these sensuous hips

The light in my smile, the curl of my lips

Take a deeper look - there's more than you see

Yet if I don't know you I may be a mystery

We all have our bad days - this I've come to know

Although deep feelings I may not always show

I am Divine, God's unique creation

With His perfect love, I am a celebration

Spiritual Revelation

I finally decided to listen to my spirit

It was always whispering the truth, so clearly I could hear it

Happiness is the key, love is the answer

Doubt and pain were spreading through me like cancer

Is love enough? That's the ultimate question?

In my own life it became more like an obsession

Everything else suffered and I hated myself

Inner turmoil ate away at me as I placed my feelings on a shelf

I placed the blame on myself for so long

Without realizing I wasn't always wrong

So I let it all go, the hurt, the pain, the anger

And I realize that I loved a stranger

I pray that God will heal my heart

And that it will no longer be ripped and torn apart

It's my time to shine and fulfill my dreams

To be the person I was always meant to be

Then maybe someday when the time is right

The Lord will send that special someone for me to find

What Love Means to Me

I was surrounded by love as a child, but felt an emptiness inside

"Silly, spoiled brat," I said, it was my foolish pride

Something was missing - I felt it in my heart

As I grew older it slowly tore me apart

The world was not as accepting of a special person so rare

For so long I scorned myself for being different - life can be so unfair

Yet as I evolved into a young woman I had ideas of a perfect love

I was so innocent yet life and love tortured me so rough

I've had my heart broken many times, it seems

And always felt that there was something wrong with me

Longing for someone to see my inner pain

To appreciate me for me and shield me from the rain

I searched far and wide, different families and faces

For the one who could fulfill my empty spaces

It is not wise to ignore the beauty in yourself

For God doesn't make mistakes and says I should share my wealth

After the latest "love" I encountered I finally see

That I can't hide and be afraid - I must be who I'm meant to be

Romantic, inquisitive, and sweet

Yet also sensuous, bold and meek

How can I be both you ask?

There are many sides to me that I will accept - life ends much too fast

So the hole in me cannot be fulfilled in another

But healed and accepted in me - I will longer suffer

I'm no longer afraid to be anything except who I am

Because I know someday God will send the perfect man

Although I've been heartbroken I long for love as we speak

But it will come in its own time - someone special I will meet

All my love, all my pain, all my passion, all my dreams

I will pour from my heart and heal through music - it is my destiny

God's Destiny

I made a wish upon a dream

Something I love that sets me free

God heard my heart and answered my call

Now I know that I can truly have it all

From Heaven to Hell and back again

I've gone through so much to be a young woman

Yet I'm stronger and much wiser, it's true

Like a butterfly blossoming from her cocoon

I've never thought I'd get my chance, yet God told me to wait

All along despite my pain, he had sealed my fate

So I hold my head up high and walk with a woman's pride

With the love of God, everything will be alright

Life without Fear

My life is coming together for me

With these mahogany eyes I can see

Although life isn't perfect, I'm happy, it's true

There are so many dreams and so much for me to do

Yet I'm healing from the inside out

To show the world what I'm made of - what I'm truly about

I don't wish to live in fear - doubt has been my companion in life

I will live the life I've dreamed - I'll try with all my might

It's all in God's plan - why am I so afraid?

He holds me in His hands - it was me that He made

So everyday I shall try to live

With joy, adventure, and love - I have so much to give

Free Expression

When I feel inspired, what am I to say?

Will the words melt in your heart from the page?

When I am sad, who do I call?

To make my world better when I stumble and fall?

Oftentimes I smile, even when I am sad

To put up a brave face and try to be glad

For what I do have in this life

Yet my true feelings I will no longer hide

The time is now for me to grow

And harvest good seeds that I have sown

Everything will come together - just wait and see

With my feelings no longer denying, I am set free

Reflections

Reflections upon this life I live

How it's changed so much in such little time - I have so much to give

A new life for me to call my own

And settle fears of being alone

I'm still alive and doing much better

I am stronger now; give up my dreams? Never!

I have so much to say and still so much to learn

A life extraordinaire is what I yearn

So I'll continue on the path that God has set for me

And always remember to live my life for me

Déjà vu

The promise of love was there

Yet you vanished like thin air

I floated high above like a sixteen year old girl

You and me in our own magical world

You touched something in me, I must admit

Ever since our very first kiss

Yet history often repeats itself

With love you must always take care of yourself

For you remind me of someone I used to know

Someone I loved who became my deepest foe

He promised the world then put a curse on me

Left me out in the freezing rain blinded, scared as I could be

I'm stronger now, but not healed yet

You re-opened my wound and now I regret

I wish I knew if your love was real

But that's a risk I cannot take - if you only knew how I feel

You're just like him - keep me all to yourself

In darkness and shadows upon a shelf

Tell me what I want to hear to break me down

I may want love but my self-worth I have found

So don't think you can change my life

Just like the day and night

I don't know if our connection is real

But I'm telling how I truly feel

The risk to lose myself again

Is just not worth it - my heart will mend

Beginning Anew

I never thought I would get over the blues

The feelings deep inside that I had for you

Never saw myself moving onto a better life

Thought I'd always hurt and suffer from your pain and strife

Finally I can feel the lifting of the curse

When I thought I'd always love you for better or for worse

But I'm happier now and never wish to go back

To that love that left me in terrible need and lack!

True love shouldn't hurt I've been told many times before

Yet I hurt so much to end the pain in my life - I couldn't take it anymore!

But God's healing power has restored my life again

And I can finally see just how much pain you did send

So I'm moving on, the time is now

With endless possibilities - Lord, just show me how!

I'll take care of myself and learn to grow

Without fear of giving up on love when I may never know

But I gave you my heart, my life, and my soul

And you threw them all away, so now I'm letting go

Someday I will love again

And pray heartache stays away so love can be my friend

So when God says it's time, He'll come along

I've learned to sing to my own song

I finally realize how special I am

And that when I can't, God surely can!

I used to envy mothers and wives

Longing and wishing I could lead that life

But life is meant to enjoy each moment, it's true

I've finally found my way - it's time to begin anew

Destiny of Ebony

The girl with ebony hair

Tanned skin and a face so fair

Had a tender, willing heart

For so many years, I thought it would tear me apart

I am older now, yet strong enough to set myself free

From the world of madness and just be me

My heart has been broken; I have fallen while on my path

And my soul felt inner turmoil and wrath

Yet I picked myself back up from where I fell before

Realizing in my life there was much to explore

Falling from depression and uncertainty, here I am

Never immortal, but still a woman

So I shall try harder, for I am wiser, it's true

Those who laugh shall fall at my feet - I know what it is I will do

My heart is still tender but still has hope

I will need this on rainy days when I have to cope

The girl with ebony hair, watch and you will see

How my path shall be fulfilled - I'll find my destiny

Reaching the Top: The Road to Success

In my life, I have always been striving for success. From piano recitals to public speaking to preparing for final exams in school, I was always running to the next goal in mind without stopping to rest and enjoy the world around me. Although I have achieved much, this was a very exhausting way to live, and I was left feeling like something important was missing: me. I was irritable, tired, and moody. That was not real happiness for me.

While I know the pace of life today is very fast, I have to take a few moments every night to take a breath and think, "How am I feeling today?" I have realized that real success means being happy where I am as a person in every stage of my life: whether I'm rich or poor, healthy or sick, just achieving a goal or working hard at it. I will always be me - that is the true essence of my success. Being true to myself and my beliefs will help me to leave behind a legacy I can be proud of.

My Realization

In every stage in our lives we will be human. Not perfect, just human. That queen, that princess, that movie star celebrity that seem to have it all "together," they are human too. No one is perfect or lives a perfect life. So stop thinking the grass is greener on the other side. Make your garden sparkle and cultivate! Make your life happier, richer, and fuller. Be brave enough to make that change.

Growing Light

I feel the light growing inside of me

Longing to brighten for all the world to see

A spark of confidence enters from the bones

As I discover and realize that I'm never alone

Where should I begin? Let's start the story

Of a shy young woman destined to find her glory

Mistakes will come, but I'm only human

It's time to move on and concentrate now on what I'm doing

The life I long to lead

All the visions in my dreams I see

That cloud my head each night and day

And vow to lift me up and take me away

God has a plan for me - this I do not doubt

The future I have begun to see with more happiness that I can count

The New Year

I'm longing and ready for a brand new start

To heal the wounds close to my heart

A new year is coming and it's time to grow

To stop and smell the flowers and let past things go

Wipe the slate clean, start over again

Praying the Lord will send that special friend

Accepting myself, the good and the bad

Realizing I'm the best friend I've ever had

Accomplishing my goals help complete my life

While I long to have friends and become my soul mate's wife

Aspirations reach the stars, yet I'll take it one day at a time

To live the life and seek the happiness God said would be mine

Darkness and Light

When passing from the darkness into the light

It can become dim and seem like it will always be night

Following the path of righteousness, you can go wrong

Pushing away loved ones until we're all alone

Fighting through failure and success

Can bring about much unneeded stress

Isolation, contemplation

Happiness and determination

The path to self-love in a fallen world is critical

The best way to get through trials of life is to become spiritual

Remain humble and you'll never fail

Although you think you're off the trail

Just hold on and remember that you're never alone

Someday you will ascend above to your true and happy home

Blessings are Near

Finally I'm beginning to see

How strong I am being me

The sun is rising and God lights the way

Blessing me every single day

Nothing is perfect but good things take time

God works within His own design

Although I long for everything today

I'm learning to trust and to do it God's way

Some days are still hard and I can fall

Yet I'm getting closer to having it all

So many blessings await my life

I pray for no more heartache, pain, and strife

Just love myself first and the rest will come

Brightening my life and shining like the sun

Reach for my Dreams

Desiring to reach the light

Dreams seem so far out of sight

In the world trying to find my place

While my heart feels an empty space

What is missing in my life?

How do I stop feeling bad and make it alright?

So many aspirations, desiring to fly

To reach my greatness before I die

I don't know where to start

Feel this pain deep inside my heart

Somehow I know I'll find my way

Replacing silence I'll know just what to say

Reminiscence of the Struggle

Success is near; I can feel it in my soul

Like a rose blossoming for the world to behold

When I feel like giving up, I remember where I've been

And how hard I had to work just to heal from deep within

My journey was dull and bleak

And at times I felt I couldn't speak

Of wretched pain that clenched my soul

And how my inner self felt so absent and cold

Yet somehow I made it through with God to lead my way

When I'm uncertain of my future, I trust Him day by day

Rising Star

Rising above the past - I can feel it coming

The fruits of my labor - my heart pounding and running

For there was a time when I'd lost hope

In living a good life - I didn't know how to cope

Trapped from one bad relationship to another

Dazed and confused - longing to take cover

I finally broke free, said enough is enough

I have a tender heart yet am learning to be tough

Loving me is the most important thing

I can do in this world to spread my wings

I'm no longer afraid of being alone

Just enjoying who I am - let it be known

I am rare, precious, and unique

Filled with love and adventures in life to seek

I know love will find me someday but for now I'm content

Being the authentic me that I was always meant

Two Worlds

I've seen both sides of the coin

As a college student and a blue collar worker that had to keep going

Used my mind for projects and papers

Worked hard to save for what I needed later

From highs to lows

I know how the world flows

I appreciate it all, the good and bad

And still work hard for everything I have

We all deserve a chance to live life at its best

Becoming authentic we must be put to the test

Nothing's impossible with the love of God beside you

Just when you want to give up, He'll make your dreams come true

The journey may be long, but happiness is near

Don't ever give up on your dreams, don't you ever fear

Mountain of Turmoil

This seizing pain takes over my mind

Stopping me in my tracks and knocking me down from behind

My world becomes a painful maze

Continuing on for many days

Shutting out my life, hiding my smile

I try so hard to breathe but the air is so foul

Wondering if this pain will ever end

Will these be a battle that I can win?

Knock down this mountain, make it go away

So I can live a better life and have more happy days

The Most Precious Moments

These are the moments in life that we can all take for granted until changes threatens their absence. The first view of the morning sunrise, spending time with loved ones, relaxing in a warm bubble bath, being snuggled up in my bed in my pajamas on Saturday morning. It's the simple things in life that mean the most to me. And I wouldn't trade them for anything in the world.

God's Divine Power

Do you ever wonder how God makes things so grand?

The creations of the universe far beyond what anyone can comprehend

Exquisite beauty of the waters and skies

He knows exactly where everything lies

From the beginning of the world to the end of time

God will truly make our lives Divine

The angels sent from up above

Witnesses and power of God's unconditional love

I'm grateful every morning when I open my eyes

Two and a half decades of living I surmise

Through the good and through the bad

God has blessed me with everything I have

The miracles of life I know God has in store for me

The future of my life only He can truly see

Contemplation of Love

Through all that I have done, good and bad

It's amazing to comprehend God is who I've always had

Though trying to open up my heart to the world

Terrifies me to the bone - yet I am His beloved daughter, His young girl

In order to pursue the Divine gifts God has granted me to do

You must open up your heart to me and me to you

Love is the answer, love is the key

Small differences separate our spirits - don't you see?

So I will be brave and remove the wall from my heart

And awaken into this life with a brand new start

United in Heaven

You look familiar to me - have we met in a dream?

My family from heaven - this life's not as it seems

I seem to recall a time and place

When we all were one in our heavenly space

Is it all in my head? Or is it true?

The fate and faith connecting me to you?

God said it was so - from life to death

We're united together to our final day of rest

Visions of happiness beyond this earth

Blessings we never conceived we deserved

This world is someday going to end

Jesus will rejoin us together - brother, sister, and friend

A New Life

We'll disappear away from it all

To start a new life - I'll hear you when you call

To awaken in the sunrise with you in my arms

Means more than I can say - I've fallen for your charms

A new life all our own

Although we'll never be alone

Take my hand and walk with me

Take my heart and set me free

I'm yours forever - look into my eyes

If you have any doubts, I'll tell you no lies

The vastness of the ocean, the richness of the sea

If you really love me, with you I'll always be

New Beginnings

With the rising of the sun, a new day has begun

To pick up where I fell and continue on my journey with the setting of the sun

I never thought this time would come, but here I am

As fierce as a tiger and as gentle as a lamb

With God by my side, I know I won't fail

Happiness shall shine, from darkness to light - I shall prevail

I'm beginning on the journey where my dreams shall take flight

I no longer have to dream, only try with all my might

So I know my time shall come, I feel it deep inside

I am stronger and wiser, it's true, from the world I shall not hide

Although people are cruel, I shall love with all my heart

From the love of God and heaven I shall never be apart

So look at me in the years to come, for inside you'll see

The wonderful woman I am - who I was meant to be

Though Art with Me

You came to me in a dream to show me of my goodness - my reward would be eternal life. Many obstacles may stand in my way, but I realize that you will always remain by my side.

I am no longer only a believer, but also a doer. That is why my life I had felt incomplete -I had never devoted my life completely to serving you because I wasn't sure if you were there. Everything good has been brought onto me by you. I am forever grateful for your mercy and tenderness, oh Lord.

I intend to leave a beautiful set of footprints upon the world and to do right by you. To touch another's heart, to make another smile; that is my calling. But I must also make myself happy - I realize that now.

I cannot believe I ever doubted you, even through the hardships, because I made it through. I have never been alone, only felt so. I isolated myself from your loving arms. Now I have cried in your embrace and accepted you as my Lord and Savior.

I am not certain I shall not make mistakes, but I intend to learn from them. Everyday is a miracle. The sun shines and the birds sing despite all the hatred and chaos in the world. Those who follow you should have no fear.

I know you are there, watching me, guiding me. Never again shall I try to stray. I may fall down, but I'll always get up again. You are with me. Goodness is inevitable.

Be Still

How much time is in this life? Sometimes I don't know

Sometimes I don't know I'm waiting for dreams to take me out of sight - always ready to shoot up and grow

Waiting for God to send me Mr. Right

And to answer my prayers and my dreams, to heal the heartbreak in my life

I can't help but want it all, although in the past it's made life hard

I have big dreams that I pray will take me far

Yet I hear a whisper from God say, "Be still."

I know He'll work His wonders and make my deepest dreams real

So as I work through all these feelings of mine

God will make everything right in His own time

What God Has Done for Me

When you feel alone, like you have no home

Reach out to God - the seeds of hope will be sown

Always remember in life we all fall

Yet God is there to catch us through it all

There are life struggles - sometimes it's hard to believe

The love of God is always near - blessings you shall receive

For when your heart aches He softens the blow

And loves you more than you could know

He holds you close on windy days

And always smiles when you pray

The world, so cruel, may come crashing down

But He's always there to keep your feet firmly planted on the ground

When you are confused, He will light the way

And when you cry He wipes your tears away

How do I know? I've fallen before

Into a world of insanity I could take no more

When I was weak, He was my strength

I felt so afraid; from ravenous wolves of this world He held his strength against

So when I tell you He is there, listen and heed my words

For he will be your Savior as the world turns

Barefoot in the Grass

I feel one with nature, as though God calls out to me

The wind on my shoulders - I feel so light and free

Free from the troubles of the world

I once again become a mischievous young girl

Eager to explore the world around me

Run through the glass and climb on the trees

So here I go boldly into the unknown

To find a place I can call home

Barefoot I run as though I could fly

As I wonder what's beyond the big blue sky

Running so far, so true and free

I hear a voice call out to me

I head boldly into the unknown

And sense that I am no longer alone

I face myself all grown up with awe

The feelings I possess are gritty and raw

I see pain upon the woman's face

The sense where love left her without a trace

Boldly we become one as hope now appears on my face

Together we can face reality with courage yet live freely through each day

Generations Goodbye

Now as we part, I must say goodbye

I'll let you go and away you will fly

You were a special part of my life

The lifeblood inside my soul I have with pride

For I know that without you I would no longer exist

And on days when the wind blows I'm reminded it's you I miss

I wish I would have known you more - you were so dear to me

We would have been good friends I know - you'll always be here with me

The last of my grandparents - it's so hard to say goodbye

Yet I know that you are happy - I'll remember this when I cry

I know one day I'll see you again, yet shine on through and through

I know you mean as much to me as I mean to you

Dreaming of Love

Where is the love of my dreams?

Is nothing truly as it seems?

I want to lose myself in your arms

Where is the love - I've fallen for your charms

I wish to run barefoot in the rain

To love like I'll never love again

Have a passion that fills my heart

An endearing love forever - we shall never part

A story out of a fairytale

An ocean large and wide for a ship to sail

Every morning as I awaken, I wonder if this is the day

When Juliet meets her Romeo and you wisp me away

I cannot help how I feel

Even if it will never be real

You never know what the day will bring

The Heavens can shine and the angels may sing

I'll keep hope alive, but love myself strong

That way I can never go wrong

My Dream

I finally dreamed that it was real

What I long for so much, how I truly feel

My dreams came to life and my soul was on fire

I was electrified by my desire

I sang with a voice so pure and true

That it was heard all over the world so brand new

My soul light as air, my fate was sealed

What I had prayed, God kept His deal

Of blessings so far and wide

It was myself that I was beside

To finally see it inspires my soul

Of true events in life to unfold

I pray that this is truly a sign

That my dreams will come and I'll truly shine!

Underneath my Eyelids

Underneath my eyelids all I can see

Is a world made of vague mystery

Underneath my eyelids, wherever I go

I can travel to a world unknown

Underneath my eyelids, I am no longer lost

Yet luring sadness makes me feel like the Holocaust

Underneath my eyelids beyond a world you can see

Surrounding my path are hidden dreams

Hidden are dreams, desires, and smiles

All to myself, yet I am still beguiled

Somewhere I know that someone understands

And lovingly takes me by my hand

Yet I am a fool, it's my imagination

An image of love made in my own creation

Underneath my eyelids, there's a secret place

Where I can go to get away and escape the chaotic world of today

My Earth Angels

Filled with wisdom, kindness, and love

They went beyond the call of duty and gave more than enough

Authentic people, real as can be

They have a place in my heart no one can see

I've been blessed by love, although my angels are in heaven

Peacefully resting on a cloud of soft ribbon

Someday I know I shall see them again

And this comforts me on days when I wish they could help me heart mend

But everything works out in time

And one day I too will see the Divine

Pieces of the Puzzle: My Regrets

While I consider myself a person of morality, I cannot deny that there are moments in my life that I wish I could take back, and mistakes I wish I hadn't made. But I learned a lot about myself through those experiences. Without them, I would not be who I am today. They have shaped and molded every aspect of my life: the good, the bad, and the ugly. Even good people make terrible mistakes.

The Real Me

For so long I've remained hidden, hidden from the world

Bound, gagged, and silenced since I was a little girl

But the time has now come for me to be who I really am

Does anyone else truly see the soul that resides in this brown skin?

I am shy and unsure of what I see

Staring in the mirror in front of me

From pain long ago that denied me my crown

Told me I was worthless and pushed me to the ground

But I am a Queen here to reclaim her throne

Stronger now and no longer alone

My soul is still sweet but my passion is like fire

I am a Godly woman yet I still feel desire

I will be silent no more! This is my life to live

I have so many dreams and so much more to give

So let me be myself and love me just the way I am

I am the way that God intended - I am a true woman

Feelings of belonging in a world unchanging

Running from mask to mask with the emptiness remaining

How did I get here? What was the cause?

Trying to pick up the pieces of life that was lost

Don't know where to begin - it's embedded so deep

Climbing so high and far up a steep

Beginning to finally speak unlocks my soul

And awakens a story that's been untold

It's time to face my fears and go for my dreams

To be human and discover what my life truly means

I will dare to live above it all

And pray that God will catch me if I fall

Unspoken Emotions

Floating between here and there

Searching for a place where someone cares

The façade of happiness is breaking down

As I stumble and fall to the ground

It's time to face what scares me the most

So I can begin to heal and truly grow

I reach out for help but don't know where to go

Who is truly my friend? And who's a foe?

The layers of protection have served me well

Yet my heart's been under a love spell

Brokenhearted, startled, and searching again

Through the fog to find a true blue friend

Hard to identify with those around me

I'm a million miles away - why can't they see?

When a queen falls from her throne

She feels embarrassed and very alone

God send me an angel to guide my way

So that I can begin my healing today

Longing in Life

Longing to destroy all the pain I felt inside

I hid deep inside my soul and cried

Longing to belong in a world of strangers

I felt as though my heart was in terrible danger

Yet God said that He had a plan for me

Something special I hadn't yet seen

So I had to have faith and this is hard

Especially when you think your dreams are nearing but they're still so far

The desire to live a life of adventure

With the security of life - yet it sometimes seems an expenditure

I must be patient and pray I won't fall again

For I must love myself through everything for my heart to mend

Anguished Thoughts

How can I describe how I feel?

When everything seems to be a lie - I don't know what is real

I hold a heavy burden on my heart

And some days I feel I'm falling apart

Amnesia of the mind, the heart, and soul

With a need to remember a story unfold

I'm grateful for God's blessings, yet cannot heal myself

I do not wish to place others again before myself

I thought one day I'd know

How everything would be - yet inside I'm hollow and cold

Lost identity with great expectations untold

As I try alone to heal myself, my story shall unfold

Please don't judge me by what you see

For truth is hidden in vague mystery

Over a decade of crying tears

With an anguished heart and untold fears

Someday I hope I'll smile from deep inside

If all could overcome their foolish pride

Someday I hope I can be whole again

And look to you and call you "friend."

What You Don't Know

You say I don't understand, yet you don't even know

The lengths I go to please you - how can love ever grow?

You were once my guiding light - my protection from the world

Yet maybe I should have saved myself - I'm not a little girl

So much to learn, so far to go

Where we are headed I do not know

I feel like I just died inside - Lord, I should have known

I took you back and hid my pride - plant the seeds that have been sown

And still months later I contemplate the path I have taken

I feel as though I've been asleep and have yet to awaken

Lord I need you, for I feel you're all I have left

Is my love still my own or is it time to rest?

I guess only time will tell the truth to me

Yet I must do what's truly best for me

Story of Sadness

The story of my life - where do I begin?

A girl once had a broken heart – now it begins to mend

She left home on a search for her soul

But of heartache and pain she never truly let go

It follows her like a shadow lurking in darkness

As people all around her are cold and heartless

The love of her life is hurting too

She's so confused, she doesn't know what to do

She longs to let go and leave everything behind

For the world has truly not been kind

Perhaps time will heal a heart corrupt with fear

Although she fears losing everything she holds dear

Always following the straight and arrow path

The world, filled with rage, pointed and created a place of wrath

Finally she followed her heart, yet it led her astray

She prays for healing and guidance each and everyday

She still continues on with a heart broken

Still not a word of pain has ever been spoken

Someday she prays her healing will come

And her soul clouded with doubt will be shined by the sun

Loving Me

In a time of life, there was a young girl

Who smiled and searched for love all over the world

Searching for a soul mate, she gave her all

Until one day her heart and soul experienced a great fall

For things were not as they seemed

And her chosen companion was not from her dreams

She thought she once saw love in his eyes

But he had been wearing a disguise

The young girl was hurt, this is true

For there was no one worthy for her to give her love to

She left it all behind, to try to make him see

Just how much she loved him, but they were never meant to be

She had gone through a hard time and needed a friend

Yet this was not an angel the Lord did send

Family, friends, and dreams she once had she let them go

But this hurt her more than she would know

She changed her image so it would be her he loved

Yet she finally realized she's perfect just the way she was

So she gave up this "love," though it hurt her so

But the time came when she had to let go

The girl learned many lessons in love

Like heartache, sadness, confusion, and mistrust

With the help of God she'll be her own best friend

And walk the path that has no end

Yet the girl knows someday true love will come

It will be sent from God and melt her heart like the rising of the sun

Until that day comes, the girl shall be on her own

Although she now realizes she's never been alone

She must take this journey, but God is always there

When it rains, it pours - how life is so unfair

Yet the love she's always wanted she'll show to herself

And longer hide her feelings on a shelf

The time has come to finally be free

To enjoy life and simply love me

Contemplation of the World

What happened to the world? Will we find peace someday?

What tragedy will take place today?

Money, the root of all evil, has taken souls away

So many wonder aimlessly and don't remember to even pray

Does God cry when He sees our pain?

Are His tears hidden in the rain?

So much must be done - I don't know why

The world has gone mad and passed me by

I feel God working everyday

And every night as I pray

Someday the end of time will be near

And I shall see everyone I hold dear

The time is now to heal the world

Although I'm only just one girl

Somehow I know it will be alright someday

And the Lord's angels will carry us far away

Madness of Life and Love

As I finally thought I was able to heal

For one step forward there are two steps back - how do I deal?

I was so grateful to be home again - it was such a blessing

Yet the past still leaves deep scars, I must be confessing

So how do I heal the broken child within me?

When I must always be strong? Why can't anyone see?

I recall where I first fell and the tears begin to rain

I was so determined for it to never happen again

Yet I felt myself begin to drown in the flood

Surrounded by despair and turmoil from my own blood

Eventually I know the pain will be worth it

I just have to realize that with real happiness I really deserve it

Darkness to Sunshine

Have you seen me fall? Have you seen me cry?

Slowly and silently wishing to die?

Enduring blows of heartache that could crush the bones

Leave you standing in the rain, cold and alone

The only way to heal is to face your fears

Don't be ashamed to run to those who are dear

The cloud of darkness wills to hand over my head

Everyday I fight for freedom, my heart filled with dread

The goal is happiness - it's a journey everyday

To see the blessings in my life that God will always make a way

So one day I believe the sun will shine its light

Banish away the darkness, my soul shining so bright

True Forgiveness

The moments of your life you carry with you. Every moment you were ever wronged or hurt - it stays inside your heart and festers whether you want it to or not when you refuse to acknowledge what hurts. For years I have wanted to release my inner turmoil. Now is my moment. It's time to let go. It's time to let the façade down and face true forgiveness. Most of all it's time to forgive myself.

Reflections of Me

Why does the grass grow?

And the truth of things never show?

I look through a mirror and see a shining face

But from my feelings I can't hide, I cannot erase

The mirror, an illusion in front of me

While distant winds sweep stormy clouds I cannot see

Where the disaster began, I do not know

I sprinted and ran, it didn't help - are you friend or foe?

I long to be a newborn babe - innocence galore

Yet my breaking heart brings me to a crashing reality I can no longer ignore

From the rising sun to the setting of time

I dream my life would be sublime

The mirror shall disappear - I'll face myself

And all the misleading faces corrupting my soul - my heart hidden from my true self

Pain doesn't stop with the passage of time

Yet it keeps growing stronger like aged red wine

I'm searching for healing - to smile from deep inside

And no longer conceal my feelings in the dark place where I hide

I must be patient - someday I'll be free

And my glory will shine true for all the world to see

A Christian's Wrath

I used to feel that in this world I did not truly belong

Blinded by my hurt and pain I didn't know your love was wrong

We were never meant to be - yet I still willed it so

Stepping off the path of my destiny - you hurt me more than I'd ever know

Your world, your thoughts became my own

And I felt so all alone

Yet now I am free - my second chance is here

With the blessing of God I know there's nothing left to fear

I have so much to say to you, yet you don't deserve my words

Your fate has been sealed - you'll get what you deserve

How can someone you thought you loved make you hate them so?

How can someone you considered a trusting friend become your deepest foe?

Is there any way to see deep inside one's soul?

To save you from heartache and lies before seasons grow old

Love and hate is a thin line, it's true

I didn't know someone could be so evil and cruel

I try to be happy, yet you step in my path

I grow frustrated and feel a Christian's wrath

But I know God will lead the way

And despite my trouble now I'll have brighter days

Wings of Flight

Wings of flight that take place in the night

What once was dim is now so bright

Heavy chains burdened me down

And held my dreams on solid ground

Yet I am finally free to fly again

This indescribable feeling is a godsend

I survived heartache and pain for many years

And cried a flood of endless tears

From behind the devastating storm rays of sunlight begin to shine

As hope dawns bright enough for me to make my future mine

Yet someday I pray the Lord will send

A husband, a soul mate, my very dearest friend

I will continue to work on me

To be strong, courageous, happy, and free

Epilogue:

The path to healing is never complete. It is always continuous as long as we are living. Growth is an inherent part of learning. Acceptance and truth continue the process of healing.

I am happy to say that although I am now where I want to be, I am not where I was. I have come a long way. Although hardships and struggles may come, God is the foundation to life-long happiness and healing.

Miracles can provide healing. I am God's miracle. I am a true testimony of His everlasting love and healing. Keep turning the pages of your life story to see where it will lead you. After all, the journey's just begun...